Keep Your Train Rolling...
Live Life Full Steam Ahead!

Jack Alan Levine

GREAT
HOPE
PUBLISHING
Coconut Creek, Florida

MY FAVORITE MOTIVATIONAL QUOTES

"Of course motivation is not permanent.
But then, neither is bathing; but it is something
you should do on a regular basis."
~ Zig Ziglar

"When I was 5 years old, my mother always told me that happiness was the key to life. When I went to school, they asked me what I wanted to be when I grew up. I wrote down "happy". They told me I didn't understand the assignment, and I told them they didn't understand life."
~ John Lennon

"Twenty years from now, you will be more disappointed by the things that you didn't do than by the ones you did do. So throw off the bowlines. Sail away from safe harbor.
Catch the winds in your sails. Explore. Dream. Discover."
~ Mark Twain

"Our greatest fear should not be of failure but of succeeding at things in life that don't really matter."
~ Francis Chan

"What's money? A man is a success if he gets up in the morning and goes to bed at night and in between does what he wants to do."
~ Bob Dylan

The Motivated Life

By Jack Alan Levine

Published by Great Hope Publishing LLC, Coconut Creek, Florida

Cover Design & Layout By Scott Wolf

www.JackAlanLevine.com
www.Don'tBlowItWithGod.com
www.LifeSolutionSeminars.com

Email: Jack@JackAlanLevine.com

Copyright 2018 Jack Alan Levine. All rights reserved. Printed in the United States of America. Excerpt as permitted under United States copyright act of 1976, no part of this publication may be reproduced or distributed in any form, or by any means, or stored in a database retrieval system, without the prior written permission of the copyright holder, except by a reviewer, who may quote brief passages in review.

Neither the Publisher nor the author is engaged in rendering advice or services to the individual reader. Neither the author nor the publisher shall be liable or responsible for any loss, injury, or damage allegedly arising from any information or suggestion in this book. The opinions expressed in this book represent the personal views of the author and not of the publisher, and are for informational purposes only.

ISBN – 978-0-9904097-6-2 Paperback
ISBN – 978-0-9904097-7-9 E-Pub

Library of Congress Control Number: 2018901800

Dedication

This book is dedicated to my Mom and Dad.

My father, Gerald Levine (also known as "Half Price Jerry"). The greatest conductor of a life train I ever saw. Dad, what a ride you had. I thank God I was on your train! It was awesome. What a blessing! Not even death could stop your train. It keeps rolling on in the hearts and lives of every person you touched!

My mother, Marcia Levine. Whose train keeps rolling even though she lost her conductor. Mom, you were always capable of driving the train yourself, but you chose to sacrifice so all your family could have a better ride. We are so grateful! Now you get to drive. I am excited to see where your train goes on this new part of your journey!

TRAIN SCHEDULE

DEPARTING　　　　　DESTINATION

INTRODUCTION	XI	KEEP THE TRAIN ROLLING
TRACK ONE	PAGE 13	WHAT POWERS YOUR TRAIN IN LIFE?
TRACK TWO	PAGE 21	DO YOU ENJOY THE RIDE?
TRACK THREE	PAGE 33	OUT OF SERVICE
TRACK FOUR	PAGE 49	WHERE IS YOUR TRAIN GOING?
TRACK FIVE	PAGE 59	WHAT STATION ARE YOU AT?
TRACK SIX	PAGE 67	MAKE SURE YOU GET ON BOARD
TRACK SEVEN	PAGE 77	PASSENGERS
TRACK EIGHT	PAGE 87	WHO'S DRIVING THIS THING?
TRACK NINE	PAGE 91	THE TRAIN TRACK
TRACK TEN	PAGE 105	WHAT IF I GET LOST?
TRACK ELEVEN	PAGE 111	SMOOTH RIDE
TRACK TWELVE	PAGE 117	SPECIAL THANKS

Introduction

Keep the train rolling! A phrase I've said thousands of times over the past 10 years. A way to remind myself and others to keep moving forward. Hey, to me there are only two tracks you can go down in life. One, lived without motivation, will definitely guarantee your life is a train wreck... literally. The other will guarantee you a life of adventure, experience, wisdom, contentment, joy, happiness, and peace. Certainly there will be some trials and tribulations along the way, but hopefully you will learn from them and it will make you even stronger for the rest of the ride. This track will enable you to look back at the end of the ride, when you pull into the last station to disembark from the earth train and hop aboard the eternity train, a well satisfied person.

So is that what it's about? Satisfaction? Yup! That's what it is about. Satisfaction comes in many forms: success, love, wisdom, freedom, relationships, financial security. I could list hundreds of words that may describe satisfaction for some people, but I believe it all comes down to the same thing... how you live your life, what you get out of your life, and what others get out of your life. That's my definition of success, and thats what I believe makes for a life filled with satisfaction.

You're just like a train. You life is like a train ride. I hope this book will inspire you to live the motivated life. It is by far the best train you can ever ride and I hope you are inspired to keep your train rolling. What does the phrase mean, Jack, and why did you say it so often? Ride on (by reading on) my friend, and then you won't need anyone to describe the sites, beauty, and wonder of life and the world that they saw from the train window of life, as you will experience it all for yourself.

How do I define the motivated life? That's easy. A life lived by a consistently motivated person. How do you live the motivated life? Let me show you. Hop on board for what I hope will be the ride of your life.

CHAPTER 1

WHAT POWERS YOUR TRAIN IN LIFE?

What powers your train? You know, some are powered by steam and some by diesel. Some are powered by electricity, and others are powered by battery. Some are even powered by solar energy. But, one thing's for sure. The train needs power to run, and so do you in your life.

So, what powers your train in life?

Is it passion and purpose? Is it survival, money, or accomplishment? Is it fear? Perhaps fear of loss? Fear of missing out? It's very important to know what powers you, what motivates you, and what drives you forward each day. And, it's very important to have something that does all of these things. The more powerful your train, the faster and farther you can go and the quicker you can get there.

I am sure you've met many people in your life. Some were down and out instead of happy. They had no purpose, no passion, and the words you might use to describe them are "completely miserable."

Others were up, excited, passionate, focused, purposeful, and driven. These are the kind of people you want to be with and who you want to be like. So, it doesn't matter what powers your train - that's an individual decision - but it greatly matters that you have power for your train.

It is critical for your quality of life to have something that motivates you to keep moving forward in life, accomplishing goals and fulfilling dreams. For instance, what if a person wants to become a baseball player, an actor, or a businessman? He may have had a difficult childhood. Maybe he was raised by a single mother and lived in poverty, and he desperately wanted to make sure he provided a better way of life for his mother, the family, and future children. That's powerful motivation!

What if your motivation is to please your mother and father and make them proud of you? What if your motivation is to honor somebody who's died - a relative, a spouse, a child, a mother, a father - and you want to honor their memory with your passion and purpose?

What if your motivation is you just love to do something? If you're a singer who loves to sing, a baker who loves to bake, a teacher who loves to teach, and you get so much joy and pleasure out of it that you would probably pay somebody to let you do it - that's powerful.

What if your motivation is to honor God with your life, and that drives you and motivates you?

What if your motivation is revenge?

What if it's selfishness?

There are a lot of motivations, a lot of different things that can power your train. However, the most important thing is to make sure you're powered. I would hope and pray that your motivation would be a positive one. It would be to make a difference with your life, to do something that you love, or to impact others in a positive way. Because personally, that's my motivation. My joy comes from being able to impact others in a positive way to help them and teach them, hopefully about subjects that are important to them. Most important to me is God, marriage, parenting, business, advertising, marketing, overcoming addiction and a host of other topics that I've been asked to teach and share on.

I get a great charge and joy out of seeing people relate to something after I explain it to them - seeing the light go on in their head, seeing them understand it. That's my motivation, and if I can turn that motivation into money, I'm way ahead of the game.

Imagine a baker who loves to bake and makes money running a bakery. Or, a chef who loves to cook and can make money operating a restaurant. Well, of course, his train is powered by the right thing. Does that mean that your train won't be powered by different things at different times of your life? No, of course not. One time in your life your train may be powered by revenge (although not a pleasant thought) while another time it may be powered by fear and disappointment, or joy and purpose. So, the motivation that powers the train can be a shifting thing throughout your lifetime.

What do I mean? Well, like the weather, things change. It's sunny in the summer and rains a lot. In the winter it's cold and windy and nasty, yet I still function and do my best. So, even though what powers our train may change, we want to know what powers our train the best. Then, we want to spend our time accessing that power.

For example, there are certain places I love to eat like Capri Pizza and Catania Pizza in Yonkers, New York. I also like to eat at the Bull and Bear Steakhouse in Orlando, or, when I want to save some bucks, Texas Roadhouse. There are certain places I love to go on vacation, like Lake Tahoe and Cazenovia, New York. I want to get there as often as I can. So if I have a choice I'm going to go where I want and eat what I want. I like Bruce Springsteen concerts, so I want to see as many as I can. I want to be in the places that make me happiest, inspire me the most, and get me excited and focused.

You want to do the same thing, so you want to realize what powers you and stay connected to, or focused on, or inspired by that position of power. Think of it as going to a gym and working out every day. You're getting stronger because you're working out and exercising every day. So you want to stay focused on what powers your train. That is a critical part of keeping the train rolling. If you don't have power, if your train is running out of power or slowing down, or you don't know what the power source is, you've got to look for it and define it. You've got to grab some power. Find some power at all costs. Discover your motivation at this stage of your life. Remember, you've got to be in the game to win it. Then find something to rally around because of course you want to be playing for the wining team.

Find your power. You've got to stoke the engine. When the fire dies down in the coal engine, we stoke the engine. When the car needs more gas, we put in more gas. We fill the tank. We hit the pedal harder to go faster. If it needs more steam, we give it more steam. Whatever it needs, we continue to feed that engine so it continues to run at optimum speed and optimum efficiency. That's what you want with your life. So, a critical part for you is figuring out what powers your train. Find out what motivates you right now.

For me, it's God. It's a desire to be happy and joyful, to make an impact on others, to have the ability and privilege to do things I love. I also like to make money (to give me the financial freedom to do the things I want) and be excited about what I do. I know when I'm happy and when I'm miserable, and you know what? My train runs much more efficiently - much faster and much smoother and goes to a lot better places - when it is running on the power of happiness, joy, excitement and motivation. It doesn't go quite as fast, doesn't usually get me anywhere I want to go, and is a pretty crappy ride when I'm running on fear, depression, lack of motivation and no inspiration.

So, find what powers your train. Plug in to it, seize it as if it were air itself, as if you needed it to breathe and use it to ride your train.

MOTIVATIONAL QUOTES

"The problem, often not discovered until late in life, is that when you look for things in life like love, meaning, motivation, it implies they are sitting behind a tree or under a rock. The most successful people in life recognize, that in life they create their own love, they manufacture their own meaning, they generate their own motivation."
~Neil deGrasse Tyson

"Whatever the mind of man can conceive and believe, it can achieve."
~Napoleon Hill

CHAPTER 2

Do you enjoy the ride?

I've flown on some airplanes that were very bumpy and flights that had a lot of turbulence, and they were crappy rides. I have taken car trips that were filled with traffic and miserable people in the car, and they were crappy rides. I have been on buses and trains that have been delayed, where the air conditioning was broken, in cars that were old and rattled with the seats not bolted properly, and they were crappy rides.

When you ride your train in this life, you want to enjoy the ride. You want it to be comfortable. Did you ever walk in uncomfortable shoes? They make your feet hurt. It's the same thing on your train ride. You want to be seated comfortably. You want to enjoy the sights, the scenery, and the beautiful countryside as you get to relax. This is your life.

This train ride is your life, from beginning to end. You don't want it to be uncomfortable. You don't want shoes that don't fit, a headache, or to feel bloated. You want to feel at your best, and you want this ride to be as comfortable as possible. So think of yourself in comfort, in slippers and a nice bathrobe, and in a reclining chair with your favorite beverage. You've just eaten your best meal and you're looking out at a beautiful view. There's this beautiful countryside rolling by and you're just in awe of the scenery and how beautiful it is.

No matter where you are, whether it's the mountains, Lake Tahoe, or the beach - whatever you consider beauty - trees, forest, green grass, farm fields, rain, snow, sunshine, as you go on this ride, the scenery changes. All of it is important and beautiful, and each scene has a purpose, to enhance your ride.

Imagine if your favorite musician was playing a concert - for me, it would be Bruce Springsteen- and you're so excited to be at the concert. You bought tickets early, and you couldn't wait for the day to come. You and your friends are excited. You're with people you love, and you know the show is going to be great.

You get there, and he comes out. You're cheering, you're excited, you're as happy as you can be, and he starts to play. You're loving the song thinking this is great. You're up, you're cheering, your fists are pumping, you're singing along, your adrenaline is at a high, your endorphins are at a high, life is at a high. You're getting perspective into life from the words, and the music is moving you. That can happen at a concert. He's playing the one song, and you know another song's coming but you don't know what it is. Matter of fact, you know he's going to play thirty songs that night. You don't know what they are, but you're so excited to enjoy that one and to hear the next one.

That's your life. Your life is that concert, and that's your train ride. As the scenery goes by in your life and the days change, turning into weeks, months, and years, sometimes the train goes back and forth. Sometimes the train comes back to locations it's been at, and sometimes it goes to new locations before coming back. Sometimes it never comes back to the same location again. But, your key is to look at every one of them, each train stop, with amazement and joy.

That's why God said we are to enter the kingdom of heaven as little children, amazed at each wonderful day. Hey, what's next? You know when you went to kindergarten or camp as a little kid? You didn't know what you were going to do the next day. You just knew it was going to be great.

"Hey, are we going to go for ice cream? Are we going to paint pictures? Are we going to fish? Are we going to bowl? What are we going to do? Are we going to sing along? Are we going to roast hotdogs around the campfire?" It didn't matter. Kickball, dodgeball - everything was great.

You were just so happy and excited to be alive and to live that day, and you looked forward to the next day. That is the train ride. And, that's why you've got to keep the train rolling. That's the critical part of it, so you want to make sure you enjoy the ride.

You want to make sure you're comfortable and you're happy. And, if you're around people who are miserable, perhaps they shouldn't be the passengers you ride the train with. If the train is going too fast for you, perhaps that's not the train you should be on. If it's going too slow, it's not the train you should be on. You should be and need to be on a train that's right for you - one that's comfortable for you. And believe me, there is a right train for every person.

You can ride in coach or in first class. What's your choice? It's all a matter of perspective. All your life you may be going down the same track, but how you view it is critical. What do I mean? One guy's idea of paradise is having responsibility and his schedule laid out before him each and every day; to another guy who loves spontaneity, that's a description of hell.

Imagine you're driving in your car and you get cut off by another driver almost causing you to crash. You're upset at the driver, you're furious thinking he an idiot and incompetent driver and should not be allowed to drive ever again! Until you find out that his infant son was dying and he was speeding to drive him to the hospital to try and save his life. Then all of a sudden, you're not mad at him anymore because your perspective on the situation or event has changed.

I believe we get to determine our own train in life. I believe we get to determine which ticket in life we buy and which train we board. Now, there are some cases, obviously, where some kids and people (birth defects, born into slavery, abuse, etc.) don't get to decide what train they board. That's tragic and sad and, to me, one of the greatest injustices of all time. Hopefully that's not the case for you and most other people. It's certainly not the case for me. Regardless of who your parents were, where you were brought up, what economic class you fit into, what education you had - yeah, there are disadvantages and advantages to all of those, but that doesn't make you a good person, and it doesn't guarantee you a happy life. It's your choice. You have to choose it.

So, you can choose the train you want to be on, and you can choose to be comfortable in your train. I don't need to have a million dollars and wear the most expensive clothes to be comfortable. As a matter of fact, there are many people who wear expensive clothes who are miserable and uncomfortable. No, I can be comfortable in department store shorts and sandals. It's most important to be comfortable inside of your heart, mind and soul, to be comfortable inside your own skin.

Bruce Springsteen said, "It's a sad man, my friend, who's living in his own skin and can't stand the company." Right. The worst thing would be riding on your train and not liking the ride. It's not comfortable, you're uneasy, you're nervous, you're upset, or you're panicked.

Have you ever been in a car with somebody who drives recklessly and you're nervous that you're going to crash? You can't relax and enjoy one minute of it. How about the guy who drives so slowly that people are honking behind him? You're in the car and you're going, "Oh man, come on. I can't believe you're driving like this." He's scared and nervous to drive and it's ruining the trip for everybody.

You want to be comfortable on your ride, and you want to be able to enjoy the beautiful ride because, my friend, this train ride is your life. And, if you don't enjoy the ride, you've blown it. You've wasted it. The purpose was to enjoy it. I know that's God's purpose, and I hope you take that to your heart. God told us that we're to be joyful always, and we're to leap and rejoice because God has done wonderful things for us. We are supposed to be grateful. Yet regardless of your personal belief about God, you should still enjoy the ride.

Different people enjoy different things. Hey, if I said to you, "Look, if you want to enjoy life, just eat pizza because pizza is the greatest food ever." Or, if I said, "If you want to enjoy life, just eat steak because steak is the greatest food." Or, "If you want to enjoy life, just move to Florida because hot weather is the greatest. I hate cold weather." "You know what? If you want to enjoy life, only listen to Bruce Springsteen music."

Okay, those things are true for me - all four of them. But they're not true for everyone else. A lot of people don't like pizza and steak; they like seafood or chicken. Some are vegetarians. Many people don't like the heat in Florida. It's mind boggling to me, but they actually prefer cold weather. I don't get it because, to me, cold weather is painful. The heat can be annoying sometimes, but to be cold is just painful. And, yet, some people love it. A lot of people don't like Bruce Springsteen's music and prefer Frank Sinatra, Lady Gaga, Snoop Dogg or Justin Bieber.

It's very much a matter of preference, taste and individuality, and that's why you've got to make sure you don't get shoved onto someone else's train. Make sure you don't get kidnapped or go voluntarily onto a train that you really don't want to be on because somebody else said, "Hey, come on this train. You'll like it."

No, you decide for yourself what train you want to be on and how you're going to enjoy it. Then you set about enjoying it and let the other guy enjoy his train. That's okay. Don't be envious. If you've chosen the Springsteen, pizza, hot weather train and another guy's chosen the cold, Frank Sinatra, seafood train - hey, don't look at him in envy. You got to make your choice, and he made his choice. If he's blessed by his choices and is enjoying them, good for him - God bless him. You enjoy what you have.

If you had filet mignon, you wouldn't worry about anybody else or what they were eating. You wouldn't be concerned. You would be just so happy that you have what you want. That's how we need to look at our lives and our trains. First of all, we should be so grateful that we have a train to ride. How lucky are we? We're alive, we're born. We've made it to this point. So many are born into circumstances in third-world countries, in poverty that's unimaginable to us and may be unconquerable. So many die as babies, and many are born with handicaps, emotional or physical, that limit the ability of their lives.

Oh, we have problems in our lives. We have issues here and there. We struggle with relationships, financial issues, health, spirituality, and with people and circumstances. Of course we do. That's part of riding the train. We'd like to say the entire ride will be smooth, or there won't be a storm during the train ride. But, yes, there will be storms. We'd like to say there will not be a time when things affect the performance of the train. But, yes, there will be bad times. Still, who cares? We need to focus on how great it is to be on the ride.

There are so many others who don't get to choose their ride or don't get to take it at all. Sometimes we take for granted the fact that we're on the train. Being on the ride, having a train to ride, is the joy of it all.

Can you imagine sitting down to eat and not being happy with the food when there are so many who are going hungry? It's all about your perspective. Our perspective - our take on life - should be, "Oh, my God, we're so lucky to have food." If we talked to a starving person or a person dying of thirst, do you think they would care what they ate or drank? No. It's just about having food or drink. But, we're so specific, so spoiled, so stubborn. And, man, if you don't get this, you missed it all. You got a train! You are the luckiest person in the world. You got a train, you got a ticket, you're in. You're in the game. You can pick your team. Now you get your turn to play. That's the joy. You get to ride the train. Don't miss it by always looking for something else that you don't have. Focus on what you have and enjoy the ride.

MOTIVATIONAL QUOTES

"I have been impressed with the urgency of doing. Knowing is not enough; we must apply. Being willing is not enough; we must do."
~ **Leonardo da Vinci**

"We can easily forgive a child who is afraid of the dark; the real tragedy of life is when men are afraid of the light."
~ **Plato**

CHAPTER 3

OUT OF SERVICE

It's very frustrating to see a beautiful new train that is broken and doesn't work. How would you feel if you just bought a brand new expensive car, and it's broken and doesn't work? You'd say, "Man, this car stinks. It's broken."

As a matter of fact, if you have this beautiful new car or new train and it doesn't work, what does it mean? It means you can't use it anymore, and it's not fulfilling its purpose. We, you and I, are trains. We'll go out of service one day. We will be useless, nonfunctional and unable to ride anymore. We would like that to happen after a life of very useful service because one day you and I will die. One day, our trains will be out of service. But in the meantime, your train is rolling.

Think of a car. What do you do when you have a new car? If you're smart, you take care of it. You keep the oil changed regularly, change spark plugs, maintain belts, water levels, brake fluid level and steering wheel fluid level. You know, airplanes can fly for more than fifty years if you just change the parts and take care of them properly. So, let me get this right. It's not specifically that you get too old to perform and you can't operate anymore. No, it's not a function of age. It's a function of maintenance. Some cars that are fifteen years old run better than cars that are two years old because people have taken care of them and maintained them properly. In order to maintain your train, you have to maintain your body, your mind and your spirit. Those things make up your train. The train is a shell built of metal with compartments, a caboose, and a locomotive pulling it. Then it has the internal guts - an engine that runs the train. So, we have a body that we walk in during this life, and then we have an internal engine that drives us. We have our minds, our hearts and our souls that drive us, and it's imperative that we maintain all three.

You've seen people with beautiful bodies whose minds are shot, and they're worth nothing. People would describe their lives as a "train wreck". You've seen people with beautiful bodies and intelligent minds whose hearts are broken, and they're worth nothing. When I say "worth nothing," what do I mean? They are unable to function the way they were designed to function. They cannot accomplish what they were designed to accomplish because they are broken. Repairs have not been made or maintenance has not been performed properly, and thus they are out of service - sometimes temporarily, sometimes permanently. Understand that some circumstances are exempt from this characterization, like physical and mental birth defects. However, apart from those exceptions and a few others, many times in life it is the person's fault they are where they are at in life. So, we want to make sure our train is taken care of and well maintained.

In NASCAR they have pit crews who tend to the car. Everybody is assigned a job - a specific task they are responsible for. One guy changes tires, another fills the gas tank, someone else repairs the engine, etc. Maintenance is done regularly and routinely throughout the race. We need to do the same thing. We need to make sure we eat properly, exercise properly, and feed our minds and hearts with spiritual nourishment. This nourishment should excite, invigorate and motivate our soul, spirit, passion, and purpose, so that being alive is a joy. Our attitude should be being on this train is the greatest thing ever - so much so that we would be scared to not maintain it because we don't want to lose the benefit of it.

Can you imagine driving along and not putting gas in your car? You say, "Well, no, Jack, I'm always going to keep my car gassed up. When it gets close to empty, you know what I do? I go right to the gas station and fill it up." Right, and why? "Because I don't want to run out of gas." Because what happens if you run out of gas? Not only is it inconvenient and you're stranded until somebody comes to help you get gas, but you can't go forward. You're stuck and you can't get where you want to go. And, there was some place you were going when you got in that car. You definitely want it maintained.

The same is true with your train.

It's not enough to just have fuel in the car. It has to be the right kind of fuel, the best kind for that particular engine. It's amazing how important fuel is to keep us moving ahead. The right fuel - whether it's food for our bodies, gas for our cars, steam for our train engine, or motivation to accomplish our life goals - is critical to obtain the success we want. The wrong fuel can destroy, derail or kill our hopes and dreams. As you know if you don't eat the proper food your body will not be healthy. You either will be overweight, have diabetes, be undernourished or lack the proper vitamins and nutrition you need.

Of course eating the proper food gives the exact opposite result. You are healthy and your body functions at full capacity. The same with gas in an

OUT OF SERVICE

engine. Premium gas affects the car's performance in a big way. The car runs better with that type of fuel. However, with regular gas, not as good. The car's performance is directly affected by the quality of ingredients that we put into our engine.

The same holds true for your personal motivation and inspiration in life. Without motivation you have no gas or steam in the engine. With it you are unstoppable. So motivation is like a fuel. Whether we desire to learn to cook, paint, succeed in business, marriage, or sports, we need the proper fuel. Just like a train needs the right fuel or steam to keep it rolling.

This is the theory of 212 degrees. You may be familiar with it as a motivational tool. You see, when water heats to 211 degrees, it gets hot. But at 212 degrees, the water begins to boil. That one degree makes the difference, and I believe it's the same with motivation to fuel your life. You may have some motivation, but if it is cold, lukewarm or just a little hot, that's not enough. We want your life to boil over with motivation, inspiration and success so that all of your dreams, hopes and goals are accomplished and realized. You have the full benefit of living a life like that, but it all starts with what's fueling the engine. So we need to make sure you have what you need - the right steam and fuel for your engine - because it powers everything and is the basis for moving forward and succeeding.

You don't want your train to break down. You don't want wheels falling off, engines overheating or stalling, and you don't want there to be a break in the track or a cow stuck in the middle of the track. Because even if your train is functioning perfectly and there's a cow there, you're stopped.

That's why you want to check the conditions you're traveling through, but most importantly, you want to check the condition of your vehicle, of your body, of your train and make sure it's running properly. You know, dementia and Alzheimer's are a big thing in our generation. I believe in the years to come we will develop cures for them. But it's not that way now.

Right now it's a big deal. So what do people do? Well, the baby boomers of my generation, who have seen it happen to their parents and know it's coming, do everything they can. They do what the experts tell them to do - try to keep their mind sharp. They do crossword puzzles, they remember lyrics to songs, and they challenge their memory to keep it sharp every day. If you don't use it, you lose it. They try to eat healthier foods with proteins that help the brain because they know if they don't maintain their minds, they will break down.

Of course, the same is true with our bodies. Obesity is a major problem in our country today. A big problem. Not only is it unhealthy and causing people to live shorter lives, but they are living less productive lives and lives of discomfort.

Short of having a thyroid issue, or another health issue that's out of your control, a lot of people can control their obesity. They can take medicine, exercise, and diet, but they choose not to. Of course, some people do choose to maintain their bodies and get where they need to go. So your job - there's no excuse - is to keep it running right. If you have a car and you don't change the oil, put in gas, change the brake pads when they need to be changed, or change the timing belts, the car breaks down. We don't say, "Oh, poor Joe, this is so sad. Joe's car broke down." No, we say, "Joe is an idiot. Joe had this great car and he didn't take care of it."

Your train is your body. That's the housing for the inner workings of your mind, heart and soul and you need to make sure you are maintaining all of these so they run at peak performance and peak efficiency. And who benefits? You. It's for you, specifically for your own benefit. And, of course, when you're at your best, you can be the best for others around you, including your family, your friends and the world, which we want to impact.

So remember, we're all going to be out of service one day, physically. Our physical lives will come to an end. I believe, personally, that spiritually we live forever. I believe that we go to heaven when we die and we're with God forever and ever.

The God I believe in, Jesus, claims that how you lived on Earth, what you did, your obedience to God, your desire to live a godly life and glorify God by being as much like God as you can - will determine your blessings in heaven. In other words, you're building up on Earth your spiritual bank account for eternity.

Knowing that, it's even more important than ever to make sure that spiritually, our hearts, our minds, our souls, are aligned properly with God so that when our physical train goes off the tracks and we are out of business on Earth, when we've served well for ninety years and run our route, we were proven dependable and reliable. We were the best train, the cleanest train, the most exciting train - a train that gave joy, happiness and comfort to the people who traveled on our train. We got people where they were going and we did it well. We can be proud of that and happy about what we've accomplished. When we get to heaven, we'll be blessed for all eternity. So, make sure you take care of your spiritual health and maintain it at all costs.

I challenge you to make maintaining your train a priority.

If it's not healthy, what do you do? Well, you do the same thing somebody decides to do when they want to improve some part of their physical, relational, spiritual, financial or emotional health. You take action to fix it. You make changes.

If you're obese, overweight, and not eating properly, you change your diet and exercise. If your car runs out of oil, the spark plugs blow, the transmission blows, or your lack of maintenance has caused a breakdown in the vehicle, you pay to have it fixed. There's a big cost involved in having to fix the car because you didn't maintain it. It's much cheaper to maintain it properly, and much more efficient. You won't be losing time, money, resources and ability to accomplish stuff if you maintain it properly the whole way. So, that is obviously the best way to go.

If you haven't done that, and you've broken down, you pay the price. You fix the vehicle, you fix the train, and you get it running properly. This time, you maintain it. Yes, it costs you more, but you're still in the game. Hey, when somebody commits a penalty in hockey and they go into the penalty box, it doesn't mean their career is over. It means they're off the ice for a while. And, what are they going to do when they get back on the ice? Are they going to bemoan the fact they just spent five minutes in the penalty box and cost their team the ability to win? No! They're going to get back and focus on the task at hand. They play the best they can to help the team win.

The same is true with a baseball player who makes errors in a game or strikes out. Do you go up to bat the next day thinking about yesterday's errors or strikeouts? No. You learn from them and go forward. The same applies when driving your train. If you make a mistake in the maintenance, in the route, in who you let ride on the train or with the comfort or climate, you fix it and move forward. You run that train as efficiently and effectively as possible.

You don't quit. You don't give up. You don't go, "Oh my gosh, I can't believe it. I have the worst train ever." I have seen so many companies go

OUT OF SERVICE

from being the worst to the best. Why? Because they change stuff. They change management, they change direction, they change focus, they change values, they change service, or they change delivery. Something changes. So, it is possible to change from worst to best, but it is a conscious decision, a conscious, clear effort. That's your job with your train. First of all, you must maintain it as best you can so you don't have issues. But, if you are having issues, fix them and change the way you do things. Run that train as best as possible. You correct the problem and keep moving forward. Remember, this is your life we're talking about!

Let me ask you something. What's better? Let's assume you were running a restaurant and the food really was terrible. Not a lot of people came, and you were losing money. However, you were prideful so you kept the restaurant open, and you could do that until you die. You'd have a crappy restaurant that nobody liked, nobody really went to, and the food stank.

Well, what if you had done that for five years and Gordon Ramsay, a famous TV chef who goes in and fixes restaurants, came in and said, "You know what? Your restaurant really stinks. Here's what you need to change." You changed it and it became a great restaurant. You had that restaurant for forty more years. Wouldn't that be better? Hey, my restaurant was terrible for five years, but then I figured out what was wrong, and I changed it. Then it was the best restaurant ever for forty years.

Or, would it be better for Gordon Ramsay to come in, tell you what's wrong and you just say, "I don't care. I'm just going to run this crappy restaurant. This is how I like it." Well, no, it's not how you like it. It may be how you're used to it. It may be what you think you want, but the results stunk and you're not happy. That's a good way to know if your train is going in the right direction. What results are you getting? Are you happy? Are you satisfied with your results? This doesn't just apply to you. It applies to the people and the world around you too. What impact, what difference are you making in the world?

If your train went out of service today, if you died, would it matter to anybody? Would anybody care? Would some people be worse off because you're dead? I hope so! I hope you're making such an impact in life and the people around you that you would be severely missed. If you wouldn't, we need to change what's happening on your train. It's never too late to get the train rolling in the right direction, as long as you have a train. Remember that.

OUT OF SERVICE

You could be driving in your car, set out from Florida to go to California, and you got lost. You had GPS but you still got lost. You asked for directions, but for some reason, you wandered around and were still lost. Remember the Israelites who wandered around the desert for forty years. For some reason, you were wandering around in the desert and you were lost. You couldn't get where you were going. And you had been wandering around for months or years, but you still want to get to where you're going.

If somebody gave you the proper direction or showed you the way to go, you wouldn't say, "Well, I can't believe I've been driving around for years. I can't get where I'm going so I quit. I'm just going to stay here and die. I'm no longer going to try and accomplish the goal." If Ben Franklin, Albert Einstein, or inventors, artists, business people, scientists or entrepreneurs like Steve Jobs, Mark Cuban and Elan Musk thought like that, nobody would accomplish anything. We all keep going until we get to the goal. That's the joy. Some get there quicker, some take longer, and some never get there. But, we all need a purpose to live for. That's the joy, the inspiration, and the motivation. That's the steam for the engine of your train.

MOTIVATIONAL QUOTES

"If you want to build a ship, don't drum up people together to collect wood and don't assign them tasks and work, but rather teach them to long for the endless immensity of the sea."
~ Antoine de Saint-Exupéry

"Perfection is not attainable, but if we chase perfection we can catch excellence."
~ Vince Lombardi

CHAPTER 4

WHERE IS YOUR TRAIN GOING?

So, where are you going? Do you know? Listen, your direction could change. A Southwest Airlines plane may fly the route from New York to Florida for a year, and then they may change the route of that airplane. It may now go from Denver to Nevada or Minneapolis to New York. It's an airplane. It can go anywhere you tell it to go.

Your train is the same way. Your life is the same way. You may have a direction for your train that you have for a month, a year, a decade - fifty years. And then you may decide you need a new direction. That's okay. It's okay to change direction. It's okay to have different goals and different places you want to get to in your life. I can tell you from experience, you will.

The things that were important to you when you were in college, and you thought would last forever, will not be so important to you at forty years old. I assure you, the things that were important to you when you were single will not be so important to you when you're married and a parent. This I know, not just personally, but by observing other people. Why do you think so many people are having tattoos removed? Oh, but I was sure I wanted her name, I was sure I wanted this candidate, this company, this song, this band, this message because that's who I was at the time, and that's what I needed to tell the world. Everybody needed to know where my train was going, but then things changed.

You could love filet mignon, but if you have too much of it you'll get sick of it fast. Things change in life. Desires and directions change. That's okay. If I have a train that's running efficiently, I can change direction. My train can take me anywhere with the right fuel.

What's the most important thing you'll ever take away from this book? My train can take me anywhere! If it's running properly and efficiently, it can go anywhere, and that's the wonderful part of your train. It can go anywhere and take you anywhere. That's why you need a train, and that's why you need to know how to run it. You need to know how to change direction and make it go where you want. You need to know how to keep it powered, how to maintain it, and, of course, you need to make sure you enjoy the ride.

WHERE IS YOUR TRAIN GOING?

You'll know when you're going in the wrong direction, and you'll know when you're going in the right direction. How? You'll know if you're happy. You'll know if you're motivated. You'll know if you're excited. You'll know if you're enjoying the ride. There's no question about that. So where do you go?

Well, always go forward. When you drive your car, it's usually more efficient to drive it forward, not backward. Go forward. Keep going forward. I know one thing. When you stop, you're stuck. And in life, you stop when you die. So, we have a direction. As a kid, we may think, "Hey, I just want to get home from school so I can play baseball." Or, today's generation, "Hey, I just want to get home from school so I can play video games." That's okay. You have a purpose. Some kids want to get home so they can play music because they're musicians. Others want to dance, sing, study science, computers or mechanics. It doesn't matter. They have something they want to do and something they look forward to. That's your train. And then you get older, you graduate high school and probably go to college and then you seek a direction in life.

Sometimes we don't know what direction we want. But, we go forward to see what things are out there. As we experience new ideas, people and situations, we discover who we are and what motivates and excites us.

Obviously cars have rearview mirrors, but you'll note they are quite small compared to the windshield... and that's for a good reason! It's much more important to look forward than to see behind. Same thing with trains. Once trains build up a lot of speed, they are very hard to stop. Trains are not concerned with the station they just left. Rather they are charging to the next station or destination up ahead. It's the same way in life. We are to learn from our experiences but we don't want to be stuck living in the past. We want to live and experience what lies ahead.

Imagine if you were going into a restaurant and had never tasted any of the food. Would you say, "Well, I won't go eat there because I've never tasted any of the food?" No. That would be absurd. You would say, "Well, let me go eat there and see what I like and what I don't like." Now, some people may tell you, "Hey, the cheesecake in that restaurant is great. That roast beef is the greatest. They make the best eggs ever." And you'll taste them and find out for yourself if those people were right. But you wouldn't say, "No, I'm not going to go eat there because I haven't experienced it." No, quite the opposite.

It's the same with your train. You want to take it to different places and see what you like. See what type of life is for you. Is it the country life? Or city life? Is it hot weather, or cold? Is it fast paced or slow paced? That's up to you, but you want to move that train forward. You want to go to these places and find what you like. You don't want to depend on somebody else. I might tell you, "Hey, this is the best way to live." And for me, it is. If you just believe me and listen to me, you'll be living my life and you'll think, "Oh, this was pretty good. But you'll never have experienced other things to know what you would have liked best because your train never went there, so you don't know."

No matter what, you keep going forward to the next place. Remember those gold miners who were digging for the gold? You hear the story and the tale of the guy who dug for fifty years and he stopped digging, not knowing he was just six inches away from the treasure, the jackpot! He stopped digging and gave up. He quit. The one thing we've learned in our world and our culture and, I believe, our history, is that you keep going and don't quit.

I certainly know that spiritually, from a godly perspective, God tells us all things work together for our good if we are living according to God's will, even though our emotions, our minds, and our bodies may lie to us and tell us other things. Certainly Satan and other people may condemn us and bring us down. But, God wants us to trust him and keep going forward. So, we keep going. Yes, it's okay to change direction. And if you don't know where you're going, it's okay to go out and explore. Be like Lewis and Clark or Columbus. Explore the world. Imagine if people just stayed where they knew where they were going. "Hey, I can't go any farther than down the block because that's as far as I've ever been and what I know."

No way, man! I remember getting my driver's license as a kid. I remember turning eighteen, and all my friends and I wanted to do was explore the territory around us, and then the country, and then the world. We wanted to see these different places and experience them for ourselves. That's your life. There may be a time in your life when you know exactly where you're going, and you should go there. There may be a time when you say, "I've been here long enough."

I was on Madison Avenue working for years, and then I knew it was time to go explore the promised land. I moved to Florida. (Yes, Florida was the promise land for me. Make sure you find yours.) I was in Florida in one area for thirty years, and then I knew it was time to move from that area to a different part of the state. There will be different times and places for you in different seasons of your life, and that's up to you.

So, don't miss the blessing. Don't be scared. Don't be fearful of the unknown. Make sure you know that you can trust your vehicle, your train, to get you where you're going and then go where you want to go. If you're wrong about a place and you say, "Hey, I thought I wanted to be here. I was wrong. I came here, but I didn't like it." Leave and go to the next place. That's okay. That's life.

You're not stuck there. You're allowed to change direction. You're allowed to go down a different track. So long as you have the train, you can keep going down the track. Remember, it's your train and your life, and you take it where you want to take it.

So, the answer to where you're going should be anywhere you want. The answer to where you'll stay is anywhere you want. Just don't miss out on seeing what's ahead. That is what living is all about. I believe you will go exactly where you're supposed to go, and you don't have to go where anybody else went. You can, but your life isn't measured by the other trains, where they've gone, how many passengers they've carried, or their efficiency and on time record. It's measured by your own train.

You're responsible for your train, not the other trains, and you couldn't be another train even if you wanted to be. You'd still be yours. You're driving in your car. There are millions of other cars on the road. You're not responsible for any of them - keeping them filled with gas, maintaining them, where they're going, or why. You are responsible for yours. At the end of the day, you get to take it where you want to take it. Don't get knocked off the track. Don't get discouraged. Don't focus on the other trains, where they're going, and what they're doing. You can learn from some of their experiences and apply them to your life, but stay focused on your train. Remember, above all, to be so grateful that you have a train. You are so lucky to have this opportunity to live. It is the greatest thing ever.

Enjoy the ride. And remember to keep the train rolling!

MOTIVATIONAL QUOTES

"Get going. Move forward. Aim High. Plan a takeoff. Don't just sit on the runway and hope someone will come along and push the airplane. It simply won't happen. Change your attitude and gain some altitude."
~ **Donald J. Trump**

"Change your thoughts and you change your world."
~ **Norman Vincent Peale**

CHAPTER 5

WHAT STATION ARE YOU AT?

Where's your train? Where does it depart? In New York, it could be Grand Central Station or Penn Station. It could be a variety of stations, but it's important to know what station you're at so you can get on board. You wouldn't be taking a flight, say from Florida to California, and not know what airport you're leaving out of. Not only would you know what airport you're leaving out of, you'd know what gate the plane is departing from.

It's important to know where your train is. Is it at the right place? Trains, cars, and planes can take you far, but you have to know what your starting point is. You have to know where you are. That's also your home base, and a lot of people ask, "Can you go back and forth on the train track?" What if your train goes from New York to Florida? Or Denver to California? That's the train route. Is it just a one-way train? Or, can you go back and forth? Well, that's a good question. Do you eat just one meal, or do you eat three meals every day? Do you breathe just once? Or do you breathe multiple times every day?

Some people live in the same town all of their lives while others travel the world. It doesn't make one right and one wrong. It's just a very individual decision on the type of life you want to lead. The answer is, it's not about how many places your train goes and how far it goes. It's about the quality of the ride and what you want to see.

So, imagine a kid growing up in the country who longs all his life to be part of big city life. He longs for the Broadway stage and the hustle and bustle of the city and Madison Avenue. But, he's stuck on a rural farm. For him, that's like hell. He's wanting to be someplace else. And, of course, the opposite could be true. Somebody who's crushed by the hustle and bustle of the city, not enjoying it, doesn't like it, might wish instead he were in peaceful, wide open spaces.

The key is not so much that you have to place your train in a specific station as it is to be in the station you want to be. You need to make sure of that. What's the sense of having the fastest car in the world if the speed limit is fifteen miles an hour where you live? Well, you'd have the capacity to go as fast as you wanted but you would be restricted by where you are. It's imperative that you have your train in the right place.

WHAT STATION ARE YOU AT?

So yes, you can go back and forth. Your whole life may be riding the rails back and forth on the train of your life. It may be as simple as a ten-mile distance, or it may be the distance of the entire world. So understand - it's not how far your train travels, it's making sure your train is going where you want to go and making sure you're at the stations and going to the stations you want to see and be at.

Hopefully no one is directing the path of the train but you. Others can help you. Certainly you're taking advantage of knowledge and wisdom and information from other people. But, at the end of the day, as the poet said, "Make sure your shoes are comfortable because you're the only one who's going to be walking in them."

I say the same thing about your train. Make sure it's going where you want to go because the worst thing I can think of is getting to the end of the train ride and having never been to the places you wanted to go on your train. Everybody gets a train. Not everybody uses it, and not everybody learns how to ride it. Some people's trains just sit there, and some never get on board to ride their own train. That's my definition of a tragedy. Some people, even though there's a train right in front of them, don't believe it. Many people don't believe in a lot of things that are right in front of them, but that's a whole separate topic.

So many people are filled with sadness and regret. Surveys have shown when dying people talk about regret, they talk about the things they did not do in life, the chances they did not take, and the opportunities they did not choose because they were scared of possible failure or the outcome was uncertain. They wanted to pursue their dream, their calling, their passion, or their purpose. Yet they got distracted by circumstances of life, doubt, lack of confidence, and fear that they might fail. So instead of even having a chance, they never even took the shot. In essence, they guaranteed their own failure by not even trying.

I don't want you to ever have to experience that same feeling of disappointment, failure or despair at the end of your life. Your train will take you as far as you want to go and wherever you want. The ride should be a great one. I want you to be able say, "I lived every mile, traveled every road, chased after every dream, loved my life, and my ride was an awesome one." That's your ticket to ride!

You also want to know where your train is stationed and where you're coming back to when

WHAT STATION ARE YOU AT?

you're out on these great journeys. Where is home base for you?

They say home is where the heart is. I believe that. The word of God says, "As a man thinks in his heart, he is." And I believe that. I believe our lives are what our thoughts make them. Your train and your ride on the train is dependent on that same perspective and that same attitude. It should be with great joy.

Think for a minute about a mailman who does the same route every single day of his life. He just delivers mail to the same local route. Now, think of a great worldwide explorer who is a mountain climber and a daredevil. Who has the better life? Interesting question. Your first thought may be the daredevil. He's exploring the world, doing whatever he wants. He's taking risks and chances - seeing everything. This other mailman guy, man, he's stuck in the same town. He does the same thing every day.

It sounds to me like the daredevil has the better life. That is not necessarily the truth at all, and it could be far from the truth. The mailman could be the happiest guy in the world. He could be content. He could love delivering the mail. He could have a wonderful family, a great wife, wonderful kids, and love his bowling league and go to his favorite rib place every Thursday night for dinner and just be loving life. He's happy. He's playing softball. He's involved in church. He's active, and people care about him. He goes out with the boys once a week. He's got a great family, and he's got a fulfilling, wonderful, happy life. He is satisfied. He is content. He is loving the train ride of his life. He knows where his station is. He knows where his train goes, what his route is back and forth, and he loves it.

The daredevil could be the most miserable guy in the world. So could the movie star, the politician, the rich man and the handsome person. They seem to have everything by the world's standards, but are they happy inside? Is this what they want to do?

Many times people are not riding the train they want to ride. They're riding a train, but they aren't happy about it. You know what? The whole key to riding the train is enjoying it.

I've always loved stadiums, race tracks, and trains. I don't know how to explain it. The structures are not alive yet they reek of life. They can't talk yet they speak volumes. They're like history books and they're alive - not physically with hearts beating, but there's something about those structures. That's just for me, personally. I just love exploring a stadium and a racetrack and the train station. I love the nooks and crannies, the tunnels and the hidden hallways. Why did you need to know that? I don't know. But it's my train book, so I can say what I want... Smile!

Different people like different things. Not everybody is fascinated by structures, but the point I make is that you want to spend your time doing the things that bring you joy, peace, and happiness. Your life is your train, and your train can go back and forth. It can go to new places, but it's your train. It needs to go where you want. The greatest tragedy would be to have a train and to never take it where you wanted it to go.

MOTIVATIONAL QUOTES

"The only place where success comes before work is in the dictionary."
~ Vidal Sassoon

"People who succeed have momentum. The more they succeed, the more they want to succeed, and the more they find a way to succeed."
~ Tony Robbins

CHAPTER 6

MAKE SURE YOU GET ON BOARD

So, all aboard! Don't miss it. What do I mean? Listen. The train rolls with or without you. Let's look at the plane schedule at the airport and the train schedule on Amtrak. Guess what? You can stay in bed. You can pull the covers up over your head. You can die - but I hope you don't. You can be sick, or you can choose not to go on the plane, the train, or the bus, but you know what? The plane, train and bus are going without you. They are carrying on. The world is moving on with or without you. News is being made, lives are being lived, games are being played, businesses are being run, love is being found and lost, and life is being lived. So, when we say all aboard, it's a reminder to make sure to live life and not to miss it!

I know sometimes things get tough. I know sometimes there are obstacles on the track, a problem with the power, or a collision on the train track. Sometimes something blocks our way - a cow, a car, a person - and the train has to stop. Sometimes the train rolls over things. Would you consider it a good trip if you were scheduled to take a flight from

Florida to California and the flight got diverted to North Carolina or South Dakota, and you never made it to California? You'd say, "No, this stinks. I wanted to go to California."

You didn't get where you wanted to go. It's the same thing if you set out on a family vacation. You pack the van, the kids, the dog. You're going from Florida up to New York and you got stuck in Georgia-weather, traffic, something. You'd say, "Oh, our vacation's ruined. We missed where we're supposed to go."

Three things have to happen in order to get where you're going. First and foremost, you have to have a train to ride. You realize it - and I say this only half-jokingly and only a little sarcastically. You can't get there if you don't have a vehicle to get you there. Second, if you have a vehicle and don't get in the vehicle, you can't get there. Third, if the vehicle is not going in the right direction, you can't get there.

So, it's important that you make an emotional commitment to ride this train and see where it takes you. Experience the journey and understand that you can't control every aspect of it. You can't see every mile that lies ahead and what's going to happen. You can plan. Others have been down

MAKE SURE YOU GET ON BOARD

the road, and you may have been down the road yourself. I took a drive up to north Florida the other day that was supposed to take two and a half hours. It took me five. There was a bumper-to-bumper traffic jam on I-75 and blinding rain. It took me five hours for a two-and-a-half-hour drive, but I made it. I didn't turn around because I needed to get there. I kept going despite the obstacles, and I got the benefit of being up there.

The main point is you don't want to miss the train. Life rolls with or without you, and at the end of the day, you have two choices. You can spend your life thinking about what to do and creating all these scenarios in your mind of what may or may not happen. If you do that you'll never get on the train, never drive it, and never get the benefit of going anywhere. Or, you can plan accordingly, make a good plan and then execute it.

Go and get on the train and see what happens. Prepare to call an audible if you need to. Hey, if I go to the pizza place and they are out of soda, I might have to order lemonade, but I'm still going to get a drink. If I'm taking a route and there's traffic, I might have to come up with an alternate route, but I'm still going to get where I'm going. You have to engage. You have to get aboard the train.

I'll take a moment now to go off on a different train track. A lot of things are going on in the world around us. Many Christians today are being shot and killed around the world for their religion, for what they believe and how they believe. Christians are being assassinated for their faith and we look on in horror. We say, "How could this be? This shouldn't happen. This is not the world as it is meant to be."

On June 17, 2015 in Charleston, South Carolina, nine of our Christian brothers and sisters were senselessly murdered in a church. They were worshipping and praising God when a twenty-one-year-old man named Dylann Roof came in and shot them for the color of their skin. His complaint was that they were African American and not white.

When I heard the tragic story of what happened in South Carolina, here's what I thought. Our brothers and sisters in Charleston were faithful in doing exactly what they were supposed to do; they were glorifying God. They welcomed that twenty-one-year-old stranger into the church and into their Bible study. They shared the love of God with him. Amazingly enough, he later said they were so kind that he almost decided not to do it, not to kill them. Imagine that, an hour with a wonderful group of loving Christians and this evil, demon-possessed kid was almost changed by the love of God. Imagine if they got to spend a day or a week with him. God's power was at work. But our Charleston brothers and sisters were faithful to the calling. They shared the love of Christ with everyone they met, even this kid who killed them. Of course we are reminded that the body can be killed but the spirit cannot. So how do we respond to this? When we look to Jesus, to our Heavenly Father, I think we realize we can only respond one way. With the love of God in our hearts. We need to love, not to hate. We need to glorify God by exalting the qualities of God: love, mercy, grace, forgiveness, which we have been given in abundance.

God has lavished His grace on us and we are to do the same to other people. We know life is a gift from God. We know every hair is numbered, and no sparrow falls from a tree apart from the will of God. Neither does your life exist apart from the will of God.

If you died peacefully in your sleep at 104 years old, does that mean you were a good person? No. If you were murdered senselessly, tragically, does that mean you were a bad person? No, of course not. It's not about how you die. It's about how you live. We don't want to see our brothers and sisters die a tragic death. We know people will die, but the circumstances sometimes shock and horrify us. We tend to ask ourselves, "How could a God who loves us allow this to happen?"

God tells us, "My ways are higher than yours." I believe God gives you life. Life is a gift. Whatever time God's given you, you should use for His glory, to build the Kingdom. God decides how much time we get.

Another difficult question comes to mind. "How can this kid do this to these innocent people? Why?" It should be no surprise that Satan, through deceitfulness of the flesh, through the sin of the mind and the desire of a heart gone astray, accomplishes his mission (which is to kill and destroy and separate us from the love of God), through a wayward soul who was trapped in Satan's darkness.

Everything that is against the gifts and the fruit of the spirit was in this kid. He was the product of a broken home. His parents had divorced at five years old. Where's his love? Love is always the answer for everything. That's what God said. He said, "I want you to love me with all of your heart and soul and love each other as you love yourself."

MAKE SURE YOU GET ON BOARD

On Father's Day, I wanted one thing, one thing only. I wanted my wife's secret recipe coffee cake and I got it. My daughter baked it for me. All God wants is for you to love Him with all of your heart and love others as you love yourself. You give God that and you have given God the greatest gift you can give Him. It's the gift of faithful obedience. In this world we live in, this fallen world where Satan's minions run wild, our job is to be the light of Christ. That's our purpose here on Earth.

I had been talking to a friend in Delray Beach about God. He came up to me the other day, after this tragedy took place. He said, "I've got a tough one for you now, Jack. How could this Charleston tragedy happen?"

I said, "How? God's ways are higher than ours. Listen, we know the script. We know how the movie ends. You're surprised that the world's going to hell? I'm not surprised. You're surprised as these signs of end times are coming closer and closer? You're surprised at the recent Supreme Court decisions regarding abortion and marriage? You're surprised at the terror in the world? Don't be surprised. All these things are coming as signs that the end is near."

Joel 3:16 gives us this great promise. "The heavens and Earth will shake, but the Lord will be a shelter for His people." He will be our shelter in spite of the storm. He has a plan for us. All we need to do is follow that plan, stay within the shelter of His wings, His loving care, seek to love Him with all our hearts, and love our neighbor as ourselves.

Every breath is a gift from God. Each second, each minute, each hour, each day, each week, each year, we're not to take for granted. We're to appreciate this gift of life He has given us.

He told us we're to do something positive with our lives (If you're a bible reader it's the Parable of the Talents). We want to use our lives to glorify God, for Kingdom purposes. He's promised if we do that, if we invest our lives in Him, we can expect to be blessed more than we can ask or imagine in this life and in the life to come.

Our brothers and sisters in Charleston didn't die in vain. They died in glory. Their deaths, and the deaths of Christians since, will rally the world for Jesus. It's happening already. They were martyrs, but before their death, they loved this twenty-one-year-old kid who killed them with the love of Jesus. It's there in the news reports. They showed him love before; and afterward, the survivors spoke words of forgiveness. What a great reward in heaven! What blessings on their souls! Is there a better way to go than praising God?

I'm not saying God's calling you to a martyr's death, but I am telling you He's calling you to a Christian life. That's the purpose of our lives, to live a life that matters for God. Could we respond with hate and revenge? Of course we could, but we shouldn't. We could respond in our flesh, but then how would the scripture be fulfilled? We need to respond in the Spirit of God with love and peace and mercy.

MOTIVATIONAL QUOTES

"I've missed more than 9000 shots in my career. I've lost almost 300 games. 26 times I've been trusted to take the game winning shot and missed. I've failed over and over and over again in my life. And that is why I succeed."
~ Michael Jordan

"Only put off until tomorrow what you are willing to die having left undone."
~ Pablo Picasso

CHAPTER 7

Passengers

That brings up the next question. Are there any passengers on the train? Who's on the train with you? Does it matter? Darn right it matters! It certainly matters who's on the train with you. You can have a great train, know where you're going, be psyched about the trip, and there can be other passengers on the train who are miserable and complaining, loud, obnoxious, or drunk. You're going to have a crappy trip. You say, "Jack, I planned perfectly. I had a great train. Everything was set. I knew where I was going. I was psyched for the journey." Yeah, you were, but you got dragged down by the people around you. It's important, to the best of your ability, to surround yourself with the right people. Surround yourself with people who are also excited to be on the train, who want to accompany you on the journey, and who have different, complementary skill sets and talents.

Wouldn't it be great if we had someone on the train who could cook meals? Wouldn't it be great if we had another person on the train who could do laundry and wash and clean? Another person on the train could play guitar. One person on the train could take video, and another person could write and chronicle the trip for us so we could record it for history? How about another person on the train who is a guide, who knows what we are going to see and can point out to us landmarks and sites we want to see as well as pitfalls to avoid?

Wouldn't that be great? Of course it would. As opposed to having six miserable people on the train who couldn't do anything, who were useless, didn't want to be there, were complaining, selfish, eating all the food, talking loudly, being obnoxious, and playing their music loudly. That would stink. Clearly, who's with us can be the difference between a great journey and a miserable journey. And, as we discussed, it would clearly be wise to have people who can guide us, who are experienced, intuitive, inventive, and exciting, who are explorers and also scientists. It's always great to have those who solve problems, are creative, and are businesslike. Now, I don't expect that you are going to have every seat on the train filled with every single discipline and personality that you would like or need. That's probably not going to be the case, but that's no excuse not to try!

PASSENGERS

What do I mean? The baseball player tries to bat a thousand. He tries to get a hit every time up. That's his goal. He strives for that, and he actually has the opportunity to do that, as every single time he is hitting, it's a possibility he could get a hit. But, as long as he has a certain level of success, he's considered a champion. As a matter of fact, in hitting a baseball if you succeed three out of ten times, you're amazing. You're a .300 hitter and that makes you one of the best in the world.

It's the same with our train. We want to put as many helpful people on the train as possible. This is the beauty of the train ride of your life. People are going to get on and off at different stations. Some people will be with you for the whole ride and some will only be with you a part of the way. That's okay. New people will come on board in new stations of your life. Your tastes and priorities may change.

Let's assume you had a musician on the train and that musician played country music. You love country music, but after a year or two of him traveling on the train, you got a little tired of country music and you said, "Man, I'd like some rock and roll or some blues or some rap or some funk." And new musicians came on the train. That would be good. You'd say thank you to the guy who played country music for a year or two. You'd say, "Oh, man, this was great, I really enjoyed your music. Thank you for being with me this part of the ride." It may be that way with a girlfriend, with a job, with a friend, or with a mentor. It may be the way with a geographic place where you live.

Or everything might stay the same for the entire journey. Again, it's your individual preference and choice. You're allowed to pick up and discharge passengers at the stations as you go. You don't want to be stuck on the train with people who make you miserable. You want people on the train who can encourage, inspire and push you to make sure you don't miss anything and make sure that the train is running as fast and efficiently as it can.

Let's say we were running a business and we had some business partners or employees as "passengers" on the train with us. We were doctors or therapists, and our goal in business was to save people's lives. I'd say, "Look. This is my train, and I want my train to save people's lives."

But the people I put on the train didn't care about saving people's lives. They cared about making money. They didn't care if the procedures they did were proper or if what they diagnosed was in the patient's best interest. They just cared about getting in and out of the room as quickly as possible to make as much money as possible. If they happened to help somebody, great, and if they didn't they couldn't care less. That's not the kind of business I wanted to run. That wasn't aligned with my dream, my vision, and my goals. I wanted our business to be profitable, but that was the second priority. First, I wanted to make sure that we accomplished our main purpose, which was to help people and save lives.

The same holds true for the people on your train. You need to have people who have your mentality. You might put people on the train thinking they have that mentality and find out they don't. That's okay. Get them off the train. Either gently ask them to leave, tell them they're on the wrong train, or kick them off because they can't pay their way in the capital that you needed. Hey, we're happy they got the benefit of the ride as long as they were on the train. But it's not a one-way thing where they get to only receive and not give. We pay to get on the train when we take a train ride, but if the price we paid was cheap, we'd think, "Hey, I got a great deal. I just got from Florida to Virginia round trip for $40. That's amazing. It's normally $500. This was great." If you had to pay a thousand dollars, you'd say, "Man, what a rip off. I can't believe they gouged me." It's the same exact trip, but what value did you receive for what you gave? We look at our train passengers the same way. What value do they provide?

I believe the people on your train should buy in to your plans, your thoughts, your theories and your concepts. They should want to be on the train and should deserve their spot on the train. That doesn't mean you won't have some people on the train who can't earn their way. You very well may. You may say, "Hey, I want to do you a favor. I want to be charitable. I want to be gracious. You can come on my train and you can ride for free. But, in order to do that, the train has to be functioning efficiently."

Remember what they tell you to do on an airplane in case of emergency. Place the oxygen mask over yourself first before helping anyone else. You have to have yourself right and operating at peak efficiency before you are fully equipped help others. In other words, what good is your train, to you or anyone else, if it's broken and no one can ride on it?

If I wanted to treat someone for free in a hospital, I'd have to first have the hospital. I'd have to have the doctors and staff in place to treat them, and, so I'd have to be profitable to do that. If I wanted to give somebody free legal advice in a law firm, I'd have to have lawyers working for me so the company was profitable, so I could do pro bono work. Your train will be a giving, joyful train. But, if the people on the train aren't on the right train, you get them off the train and continue to look for the right people to be on the train. Remember, the one thing you've got to do is keep the train moving forward.

You don't stop and wait for the ideal circumstances. You go forward. If things slow down, you figure out how to speed them up. And, if there are obstacles, you deal with them (by figuring out how to overcome them or go around them) and look to try and develop the best possible passengers on your train to make the ride as enjoyable as possible. You know, just like the baseball player who says, "Look, I may not be able to get it perfect, but I can get really close. And, if I get close, it will be amazing." So, remember, it's not about perfection. It's about striving for that goal. It's about progress, live like that and you will find the journey amazing. Having the right passengers on the train is critical.

Here's the great news. It's your train. You get to pick the passengers. In your house, you get to decide what guests come and go and how long they can stay. You actually get to dictate their behavior because many times that determines whether you want them in your house or not. You get to examine who they are and decide if you're going to invite them in. And sometimes, when you're not sure and you invite somebody in only to find out who they are, how they behave, and what they think, you'll decide if you want them to stay or go. You can decide whether you ever invite them back again.

Your train is the same way. Certainly, you wouldn't want to be miserable in your own home. That's a place of refuge and joy, a place where you want it to be as you created it. It's a place you can control, and you want your train to be the same way. You want your life to be the same way as much as you can, so you want to surround yourself with people who are excited to be on your train and are willing to carry their share of the load. You want people who share the same desire to have a great journey and get to the same destination. You understand, of course, that people's minds and perceptions can change along the way and we may have to alter who's on the train and off the train at any given time. But we want to look for talent, passion, unity, like-mindedness, and whatever it takes to move that train forward in the most positive, effective way.

One last thought on that. When I say like-mindedness, it doesn't mean any two people have the same personalities, or we all like the same sports team or the same music. No, it means we share a common goal and we sacrifice for that goal to get to that destination or to live a life of joy, purpose, focus, or passion. We share the drive to create or to accomplish, to engage or to encourage, to inspire or to impact, or to change the world or to enjoy it. You've got to have a passion and a purpose in your life. You've got to have a reason for riding that train. When we see somebody who lives their life aimlessly, without purpose, and wandering about, we say, "Oh, what a waste. What a loser. Man, the guy accomplished nothing. He had a train, never drove it, never used it, never cared where it went." How sad is that? That's not going to be you or me. So make sure you've got the right passengers on the train.

MOTIVATIONAL QUOTES

"Do it or not. There is no try."
~ Yoda

"The way to get started is to quit talking and begin doing."
~ Walt Disney

CHAPTER 8

WHO IS DRIVING THIS THING?

Who is the engineer of the train? Is it you or somebody else? Hey, I may be the driver. I may have the steering wheel. I may be the owner of the railroad company and get to decide where the train goes, but I want a good engineer on board. I can be a great musician, but when I get into the studio, I want a great engineer who can make the sound and the voice come out as clearly as possible so the end product is as good as possible.

I want an engineer on that train who can make that train run as efficiently as possible, as effectively as possible. I want someone who knows how to successfully navigate the turns, when to slow down on mountainous turns and when to speed up, and who knows how to read all the railroad signals. I want an experienced engineer who can get me where I'm going in the most efficient and comfortable way possible. Wouldn't you say the same for an airline pilot? Wouldn't you want somebody who knows the routes, how to handle turbulence, what to do in an emergency situation and how to handle weather so that your flight is as comfortable as possible?

How do you know? How do you know who the engineer should be? How do you know what people you should have on the train? Well, there's a couple of different ways. I'd want my engineer to be skilled, capable, and experienced. I'd want him not to be drunk or reckless because my life is at stake. I look for certain qualities in a engineer candidate just like I do with the people on the train. I'm looking for people who are enthusiastic, encouraging, supportive, and who will not knock me down but will build me up and point out to me what I'm doing wrong to help me be better. Mentors, friends, family, acquaintances, and professionals can all serve as engineers at one time or another. You may be the engineer at some point in time. But one thing for sure, someone who knows what they are doing should be driving the train.

I desire to be better and accomplish more so I want an excellent engineer. I also want people on my journey who want to be there, who are excited about the journey, and who have the same goal and purpose at that point in my life when I'm driving the train.

MOTIVATIONAL QUOTES

"Successful and unsuccessful people do not vary greatly in their abilities. They vary in their desires to reach their potential."
~ John Maxwell

"The whole secret of a successful life is to find out what is one's destiny to do, and then do it."
~ Henry Ford

CHAPTER 9

THE TRAIN TRACK

You know the train track is the road of life. It's the road you go down. As we said, there will be stops, slowdowns, and changes. You'll hear the train whistle, which is a beautiful sound. You can hear it coming from a mile away. It makes an impact. It's loud when it roars through.

That's how our lives should be. We should make an impact. We should be loud. I don't mean obnoxiously loud; I mean loud in a way that's impactful and matters in life. Not quiet and invisible when nobody sees us and our lives don't matter so that it wouldn't matter if we're alive or dead. Oh, it might matter to us as we satisfy our selfish desire for food and pleasure and stuff, but it doesn't matter to the world. Our lives should matter to the world.

You know what the beauty of a train is? It does something very important. It gets people where they want to go. That's why they get on the train. They're here and they want to go there. They need the train to take them. Your train, in your life, should take you where you want to go, and it should be loud and beautiful and thunderous as it steams ahead full speed. When it stops at the station to let people off or pick people up, people say, "Oh, wow, look at that train. Look at that locomotive. Look at how it operates so efficiently and effectively and beautifully. It's a well-oiled machine." That's your train. That's your life.

When the train's late we get mad. We say, "Hey, where's the train? I'm sitting here waiting. How come it's not on time? What's wrong with those guys? Why can't they get the train here on time? Why don't they have their crap together? They stink. They are terrible." That's right, we say the same thing about planes, cars, businesses or people. So, we want our train to run efficiently and effectively - to do what it's supposed to do so that it affects people in a positive way and has a purpose. We want our train to make a positive difference in the world.

Okay, so I know you've figured out by now that the train is a metaphor for your life. I've said it multiple times, but it's more than that. It's an attitude and a way of life. It's almost like a slogan, a rallying cry. It's a life verse, like a mission statement.

THE TRAIN TRACK

"Keep the train rolling."

That's your job, your purpose - to keep it going. Keep it moving forward so it can be that vehicle to get you and others where you want to go. It can be the greatest ride ever. There are a lot of ways to travel. You can walk, you can hitchhike, or you can go on horseback. You can drive, take the train, take the bus, or fly. The day is coming where you'll be able to jetpack from place to place. There are a lot of ways to travel. Some people like certain ways and some like others. You need to travel and live the way you prefer to keep your train rolling. You need to roll regardless of if the weather's good or bad, whether people are grumbling or happy, whether it's dark or it's light, whether it's hot or it's cold, and whether the wind is with you or against you.

Like when you drive at night and you can only see about a hundred yards in front of you from the light of your headlights. You will never at any one time ever see further than the headlights allow you to see. So you will never be able to see more than one hundred yards in front of you at the most. But you can go the whole trip that way. You don't need to see beyond the light of your headlights as they light the way in front of you as you go. Sure it would be nice to be able to see the whole road lit up for the entire length of your trip from New York to California, or see your whole life's path from beginning to end, but it doesn't work that way. We have to live one moment, one day at a time, making the most of each moment and each day, making the most of each mile and each stop on the train.

All I know is some days you'll go faster than others, and some days you'll get farther than others. Sometimes you'll want to stop and see the sites. All that's good, but you can't stop the train from rolling. You can stop to pick up passengers in the station - that's not what I'm talking about - but you can't stop the train. You've got to keep it moving forward. This is the key to life. Keep the train rolling.

People live and die. People come and go. Opportunities come, health comes, money comes, and relationships come. Sometimes we're happy, and sometimes we're not so happy. Sometimes the food's good, but sometimes it's not. Sometimes we make money, and sometimes we don't. Sometimes people like what we say, yet other times they don't. Sometimes our friends are friends forever, and sometimes they're friends until we say something they don't like. Unfortunately, it can even be the same with our family.

THE TRAIN TRACK

You can lose everything - your money, your health, your house, your property, even your family. All this stuff can be taken, but they can't take your heart, soul, mind, and your relationship with God, if you have one. You were given this one life, this one train to ride here, on Earth. I believe we'll be in heaven with God for all eternity, and that's a different story. But, for right now on Earth, we've got this one train to ride. I have realized that in order to make the most of my life, in order to live the best life, I must have the best ride I can. I have come to the conclusion that there's only one thing I have to do. I have to keep the train rolling - whatever that entails.

One day it may entail putting more fuel in the train, feeding in more coal or steam or diesel. Another day, it may require repairing a train track up ahead. It may require different passengers. Another day it may require new supplies or other things, like better engineering or just more focus. There are so many things involved in making the train roll, but my job is to keep it rolling. It is my responsibility to keep my train of life moving forward.

However I'm reminding you again, when you're broken down, you can't go anywhere. You know what we say when someone's broken down? We say they're stuck. "Hey, I'm stuck. Come help me. I broke down. I can't get out of here. I need help. I'm stranded."

A lot of people feel that way in their lives when their train stops. But, see, for most people, they don't get that they control the train. It's their responsibility, their obligation, and it should be their desire and joy to make sure their train keeps rolling. They must do whatever is possible to make sure that train keeps rolling. Somebody you love may have died. You may have lost something valuable to you. You may have made a bad investment decision or a bad business decision. Maybe you were fired from a job that you thought you had for life. Somebody you love may have broken off a relationship with you or be mad at you. Somebody's not listening to what you say - a child, spouse, friend or boss. You don't feel well - a headache, a stomach ache, or perhaps a more serious illness.

You've got to keep the train rolling. That's the only way to keep moving forward. If you break down and you're stuck or stranded, you can't go

THE TRAIN TRACK

anywhere. It's over. And that's the importance of keeping the train rolling. There are a lot of parables in life. There is the power of positive thinking and the spiritual aspect, which says, "Keep the faith." There's the slogan, "Winners never quit, quitters never win." All of these things from different parts and spheres of life inspire you to do the same thing - keep going, keep pushing ahead, keep running the race. They motivate you to never give up.

"Keep the train rolling..." I use it as a greeting. I use it instead of saying good-bye, aloha, or God bless you. I usually end my conversations, my phone calls, my letters, and my face-to-face meetings with this simple phrase. And, of course, people say it back to me now, because they know it has meaning to me, and they get the meaning. Then it starts to have meaning to them. Keep the train rolling... It means hang in there. Don't give up. Never quit.

The greatest comebacks I've seen in sports and in life were from people who kept going when all odds were against them, when it seemed as if they were defeated, stranded, dead, broken down, beaten- lost everything. And, in many cases they had. This was a reality. They had lost physically, emotionally, spiritually, financially, relationally and yet instead of saying, "Hey, I am done with this ride. If this is where the train has taken me, if this is how the train rides, or if these are the people on my train, I'm not going to be on it. I'm off the train," No, they kept going.

When you knock your king down in chess, you're done. Your game's over. When you walk off the field in the middle of a game, you quit. You can't win anymore. You've taken yourself out of the game. That's right, you've taken yourself out of the game. I believe there's a spiritual enemy, Satan, who would love to take you out of the game and get you discouraged any way he can to take you out of the game. And, I believe there's God, who wants you in the game no matter what. He wants to remind you that He's with you and loves you. There's a purpose and plan for your life. There's a place in heaven for you when your time on Earth is done. I believe God is saying, "You know what? I want you to ride this train, which is your life, and enjoy it. Let your train be a train of impact to help others. Have a train that matters and has a purpose. You fulfill this purpose."

Imagine a police officer who didn't step in and stop a crime when he saw it or didn't help a citizen. We'd say, "Man, you're a failure. What a loser. You had a purpose and you didn't do it." Or, imagine a surgeon, who had the skills to save somebody's life

THE TRAIN TRACK

and refused to operate because he was tired or didn't think the person was worth it. Maybe he didn't give it his best and didn't care. We'd say, "Oh, what a bum. Man, we hate you. We can't believe you're that way." Right. We have a purpose, too, and we just need to try our best.

Any of you who are parents know that you don't hold all your kids up to the same standard of achievement. No, you look at them individually. You want them individually to be the best they can be and give them the opportunity in life to reach their maximum capacity and fulfillment. You want to see them have joy and be happy.

It doesn't mean they all have to be doctors or lawyers - no. Some may have that capacity, and that's great, but it's an individual accomplishment for each child based on their abilities, passions, and desires. Basically, it depends on the way they were wired, made, and created. Part of that comes from their gene pool, and part of that is spiritually, from their hearts and minds.

God looks at us the same way. We're not measured against other people and what they accomplish. We're measured against our potential. We're not measured in terms of pass or fail. We're measured in terms of opportunity given. God wants us to have the same opportunity. We all have a train, and we all have the ability to keep that train rolling through this life and have it be the greatest journey ever. Yes, ever!

There will be thunderstorms, snowstorms, earthquakes and hurricanes in life. I get that. It's part of the journey. There will also be sun-filled days and amazingness, and there will be a lot more amazingness and sun-filled days than there will be storms. But, when you ride out the storm and learn how to navigate through it, you gain skill and experience, and you have even more appreciation for the sun-filled days and the joy-filled days. But, you also know that, "Hey, I can ride through this storm. I might not like it, I might not enjoy it, but I am skilled."

I have driven in snowstorms and blinding rain, and I'm not saying it was fun. Quite the opposite, but because of and through that experience I've acquired heightened driving skills over the years. I have confidence in these situations. Even though I don't like them, I feel like I'm a confident, competent driver. I can handle these tough driving situations carefully and skillfully with assurance of the outcome.

THE TRAIN TRACK

That gives me confidence when the storm comes. I don't want the storm, but I know I can go through it. I know my car is not going to break down on me because I've taken care of it. I have confidence. I know how to drive and I can get where I'm going.

I want you to have that same confidence in your life. I want you to have that same joy and excitement that life is a gift. It's a present, and I can get anywhere I want to go. I can do anything I want to do. I'm only limited by my imagination and the boundaries I mentally set for myself because, for most of us, there are no boundaries. We're not in prison. The only prisons we're in are the ones we set in our minds. The only limitations we have are the ones we create for ourselves. The world hasn't placed limitations on us.

Other people may have placed limitations on us by their judgments or thoughts, but they don't count. They don't get to decide what I can or can't do, where I will or won't go. They may have an opinion, a statement or a point of view. They may not think I can do it or have confidence in my ability, but their thoughts do not dictate my actions or outcomes. My thoughts and my actions control my outcomes. Their train does not dictate where my train goes. My train may be side by side with theirs.

They may be ahead or behind or on a different route, but that's their train. They can point at my train, make fun of my train, think it's great, think it's bad, but you know what? I'm responsible for my train. Not them. I control the forward movement of my train.

Can you imagine if a ball player in the stadium refused to get up at bat because people were hollering at him? Or said, "I quit. I can't play anymore because the fans think I stink because I made a few errors." We'd say, "Man, that's ridiculous." We know they're out there yelling at you and saying you stink, but you're supposed to be able to handle that. You're a professional. You're supposed to be able to play, concentrate, and focus on the task at hand and not get distracted by what others are saying or doing, or what the crowd is cheering or chanting.

If you get distracted by that, we say you have no focus and no concentration. You have "rabbit ears," and you're letting them get in your head. We know that is never a good thing. So remember, you are responsible for your own train. Nobody else. You. Don't go blaming other people, the world, circumstances, or anything for the fact that your train is not going where you want or is not on the right track.

MOTIVATIONAL QUOTES

"The successful warrior is the average man, with laserlike focus."
~ Bruce Lee

"Success is walking from failure to failure with no loss of enthusiasm."
~ Winston Churchill

CHAPTER 10

WHAT IF I GET LOST?

What do you do if you're driving and get lost? You ask for directions to start heading in the right way. Either you look at your GPS in this day and age or you Google it. In the old days, we would stop and ask for directions. Why? Because once I knew I was lost or off track, I didn't want to keep going in the wrong direction. I didn't purposely get lost, but once I realized I was, my immediate goal was to get back in the right direction. That needs to be your goal, and your plan is to get back on track. Why should I get back on track? So I can keep the train rolling. Why should I keep the train rolling? So I can get where I want to go. Most importantly, and please, if I've taught you anything through our time together in these writings, remember to enjoy the ride.

Live with passion, purpose, joy, peace and love. I understand you're going to have a tough day here and there, but our goal is to have every day of our life be great. If we are successful most of the time we will have the most amazing life ever. It's a beautiful train. It's a beautiful day. It's a beautiful world. It's a beautiful life. You can choose to look out that window and see the countryside and the cities as they roll by. You can stop and greet the people as you get off the train and explore the towns around you. You can get back on the train and engage and interact with the world, or you can choose to hide from it. You can choose to close your eyes, or look down, so you can't see anything. You can shut the world out, or you can let it in. Either way, you're going to live your life.

One of those ways, I believe, is full of darkness, pain, frustration, anxiety, depression, sadness and I'll just call it a lack of joy. That's the way when you choose to shut the world out. I do not believe that is a way to have a joyful life. The way I believe is best to have a joyful life is to look at the world and engage it. See it and interact with it. Yes, it's not perfect. Yes, there are bad people. Yes, there are problems along the way. But, that's a small price to pay for getting to ride the train.

Keep the train rolling and live and enjoy this wonderful gift of life that we have. You know, many things are inconvenient, yet we do them without thinking. We go to the supermarket to get food. We shop. We pump gas in our cars. We do a lot of things that seem inconvenient, but we do them for one particular reason - because we want the end benefit. We deal with the inconvenience of supermarket shopping because we want the benefit of the food we buy. We go through the cooking process because we want the benefit of it. It would be better if it just appeared before us, but it doesn't work like that for most of us.

It is the same when working to make money for the things you want to do. The same thing with raising kids and investing in relationships. There's inconvenience, and there's work involved. Some of it we don't want to do, but we do it to get the benefit of it, to get the end benefit, and that's why you want to keep that train rolling. You want to enjoy the ride and the benefit of it. You want the satisfaction of fulfilling your purpose.

My last point is this: You are responsible for doing whatever it takes to keep your train rolling. If your train is not functioning properly, you're responsible for finding a repair guy. If the air conditioning broke in your house and you couldn't fix it yourself, you would call a repair guy. If your plumbing broke and your toilet was backed up, you'd try and plunge it. If that didn't work or you couldn't do that, you'd call a plumber. You'd do whatever it took because you couldn't live with broken plumbing.

Hunters and cave men in the old days hunted for food. They left their caves and hunted for food so their families wouldn't starve. They did whatever it took, and that's what you need to do - whatever it takes.

MOTIVATIONAL QUOTES

"Don't be afraid to give up the good to go for the great."
~ John D. Rockefeller

"All our dreams can come true if we have the courage to pursue them."
~ Walt Disney

CHAPTER 11

SMOOTH RIDE

Some of you will have easier rides. Some of you will be so fortunate that there won't be so many storms, obstacles, interruptions, or unruly passengers. Some of you will figure out quicker how to make the train run smoother, and some of you will take longer. But it doesn't mean you don't try. It doesn't mean if you failed your driver's test one time you say, "Well, I'm not going to get a driver's license."

What if you fail three times? You don't say, "I'm not going to get a license." No, you keep taking it until you pass. Even if it's eight times. Why? Because you want the benefit. You have to have that driver's license. You want it. And you know what the beauty is? When you get it, nobody ever says, "How many times did you take the test?" The only question is, "Do you have the license or not?" That's the only question at the end of the day. So, the only question at the end of the day for you is, "Did you keep your train rolling?"

Man, roll that train. "Laissez les bons temps rouler" - let the good times roll. Let your life be that train. Keep it rolling. Make an impact. Do what it takes because it is so well worth it. This is what living is. People spend their whole lives looking for the purpose of life and meaning. Of course, I believe that comes from God, but there's also an earthly answer and a practical answer. That answer is, "This is the time we have." This is your train. Keep it rolling. Go forward. Choose the track and leave the station.

Be open to change, progress, and innovation. If new wheels come, or new technology comes to move the train faster or better, adopt it. Don't get stuck in the past. Be open minded. But most of all, enjoy the ride. You should consider it a blessing that you have a train to drive, that you have a life to live. Otherwise, it won't matter what you have, what train you have, or who is around you because you're going to be miserable. Living life is about being grateful. It's about gratitude. It's about appreciating life as a gift and enjoying it.

So, my friends, this was your "train"-ing manual. Ha-ha, get it? I believe each one of us has within us the keys to the universe. We have the engine to the train, and it is internal, inside of us. It is in

SMOOTH RIDE

our hearts, minds and souls when they combine to function properly to look at life and people as things to be cherished and loved, helped and encouraged, and to bring joy from being a vehicle that gets people moving forward. We want to be those trains for other people. We want our lives to be the trains that kept rolling, lifted people up when they were down, moved people forward, took people where they needed to go, gave them great pleasurable rides, mattered in their lives, and functioned in an effective way that brought them joy, excitement, and happiness. We were dependable, reliable, on time, and efficient. People could count on us.

You and I are conductors of our trains, the engineers, the owners, the riders. You and I did everything we could to make sure that our train was available, accessible, and accomplished what it was created to do. I pray that you do what you were created to do in your life. I pray that you would realize that you were created to love others, to be an impact player in this life. Your job is to ride your train and make sure your train - the life that you live, the train ride that you've been given, the route that you've been given - is the best possible train. Make sure you're the best conductor and the best engineer. Make sure your train is the best so that every single person who rides that train will say, "Man, what a great train. You've done your job well." You can rest assured that I believe you will be rewarded and blessed for that for all eternity - for your faithfulness, for your appreciation of the gift of life you've been given, and for your desire to be the best you can possibly be.

My last words to you are not a surprise. I'm sure they're exactly what you'd expect, and I hope they have more meaning to you now than ever. I hope you'll adopt them as your own and be blessed, so, **"KEEP THE TRAIN ROLLING" AND YOU WILL LIVE THE MOTIVATED LIFE!**

MOTIVATIONAL QUOTES

"The only person you are destined to become is the person you decide to be."
~ Ralph Waldo Emerson

Special Thanks

My wife Beth. My wonderful children, Ricky (Kristi and Harper), Jackson and Talia. Thank you for making my train ride the greatest one I could ever imagine. I cannot imagine riding the train without any of you on it. You have each individually and collectively provided me with the greatest fuel of all to live and enjoy life, and that is the fuel of love and inspiration. I am so grateful. Love you guys.

Amanda Brown. Perhaps the greatest living editor ever (certainly in my opinion).

Scott Wolf. The king of design. You really are creative genius! I hope you know it. (Rest assured I know it!)

Shaun Smith. Thanks for continuing to help with my books, projects, archives, ministry, conferences, seminars and all that you've done for me through the years behind the scenes. I'm extremely grateful for your friendship, love and support, but most inspired by your faith and trust in God.

Keith Greiveldinger. Thank you for proofreading and some very helpful insight. Keep winning each day.

All my love.
Jack

CHECK OUT

LIVE A LIFE THAT MATTERS FOR GOD

"From a clinical perspective, *Live a Life That Matters for God* has great value as a teaching and therapeutic tool for the soul. From a spiritual perspective it is a direct hit right to the heart of every Christian. This uplifting book will inspire you no matter what chapter you are reading. I love that you can pick up any chapter, anywhere, in any section in the book and be blessed immediately. Jack covers so many different topics that are relevant and critical to our growth as Christians, our happiness and our desire to walk closer with God. Jack's style is straight to the point and laser focused. Jack doesn't just tell you to do it, he shows you how!"

Julie Woodley,
MA, Division Chair American Assoc. of Christian Counselors

WHERE THE RUBBER MEETS THE ROAD WITH GOD

For every believer who wants to make sure they hear "Well done good and faithful servant."

"A knock out punch for Jesus if there ever was one. Jack Alan Levine's book is the heavyweight champion of the world when it comes to Christians walking a life of faith with God. Read it and make certain you will wear the champion's crown of life for Christ."

Nate "Galaxy Warrior" Campbell,
3x Lightweight Champion Of The World

DON'T BLOW IT WITH GOD

In *Don't Blow It With God*, Jack Levine reveals his road map to discovering God's blueprint for living the ultimate Christian life each and every day. Come along for the ride as God teaches Jack life-changing lessons that will help you in your life journey. Jack discovers how to live an abundant Christian life experiencing true joy, peace and happiness and along the way you will discover the formula and the insights about how you can too.

"Jack's unique style of communicating God's plan for an abundant life is a must read for all Christians. This book knocks it out of the park. If you've been striking out and want your life to be the perfect game for God then you need to read this book."

Chris Hammond, Major League Baseball pitcher

MY ADDICT YOUR ADDICT

This book is about addiction. Author Jack Levine has counseled thousands of people over the years who have gone through addiction, and knows what a torturous life it can be to be caught up in it. It's an awful thing.

He's experienced addiction in his own life and as a parent, as he watched his son struggle with addiction for years (it started when he was 18).

Whether you are in the throes of addiction yourself or seeing a loved one suffer through it, this book can help you. Jack has results and solutions for real-life situations. Each person's situation is different, but the root is the same for everybody. Through his own story, he can tell you what the choices are, the impacts of those choices, the results of those choices, and what sacrifices you'll have to make to get where you want to be.

JACK'S OTHER BOOKS...

DOWNLOADING GOD

"*Downloading God* is the file of information that today's generation needs to click on more than ever. Jack Levine's authentic and transparent self-disclosure rings through in his passionate devotion to his Lord and Savior Jesus Christ. His simple, straightforward, trademark writing style as in his previous books allows the reader to easily absorb, appropriate and apply the word and truth of God in a realistic, revolutionary and redemptive way. 'Downloading God' has short chapters all themed around a clever computer technology motif which makes the timeless truths of God both real and relevant to contemporary culture."

Dr. Jared Pingleton, VP American Association of Christian Counselors, Clinical Psyhchologist, Credentialed Minister

TIME GONE

Each year we like to send a holiday letter to our friends and loved ones looking back at the past year and looking forward to the coming one. These letters are extremely personal but also extremely universal. Though written at holiday time, the observations I share are a true reflection of life all year long. In them I share my struggles, joys and thoughts, which like yours, change from year to year and I'm sure mirror many of the same things you go through.

I've left some personal things in here to give you a sense of who I am - a regular person like you with all the normal victories, defeats, happiness, sadness, joy and pain that we all share. Each letter contains reflections, lessons learned, wisdom and insight that God laid on my heart that particular year. I believe these will help you with your life and have great value to you. In these annual holiday letters I ask people to stop, take stock of where they were at, and consider how they were going to move forward. I hope that by sharing these letters with you it will cause you to do the same.

PIECES STILL GOOD

His writings emanate from questions like Who am I? What is the purpose of life? As well as the suffering, pain, realizations, romantic breakups, and uncertainty regarding the course of his future. Jack's intense feelings are reflected in his poetry. Although not all of it was pleasant and he is embarrassed by some of these writings, Jack publishes them all, unedited, leaving nothing out, so you truly walk with him through this phase of his life.

There was torment, confusion, frustration, dissatisfaction, fear, and greed, along with a host of other feelings... And then a transition to a better way of life, a life filled with peace, joy, hope, happiness, mercy, love, and kindness. Jack's goal is to inspire his readers, make them think, and most importantly serve as an example.

LEARN MORE ABOUT JACK

JackAlanLevine.com

www.ingramcontent.com/pod-product-compliance
Lightning Source LLC
Chambersburg PA
CBHW050437010526
44118CB00013B/1576